DOGS SET XI

WEST HIGHLAND WHITE TERRIERS

Kristin Petrie

ABDO Publishing Company

Cover Photo: Alamy
Interior Photos: Alamy pp. 5, 15, 16, 18; Getty Images p. 11; Glow Images p. 17;
    iStockphoto p. 9; SuperStock p. 7; Thinkstock pp. 12, 13, 19, 20, 20–21

Editors: Rochelle Baltzer, Megan M. Gunderson, Bridget O'Brien
Art Direction: Neil Klinepier

Library of Congress Cataloging-in-Publication Data

Petrie, Kristin, 1970-
  West Highland white terriers / Kristin Petrie.
      pages cm. -- (Dogs)
  Includes index.
  ISBN 978-1-62403-103-8
1. West Highland white terrier--Juvenile literature. I. Title.
  SF429.W4P48 2014
  636.76--dc23
                    2013025487

CONTENTS

THE DOG FAMILY

Dogs! Some are big, and some are small. Many dogs are hairy. A few are hairless. Some dogs are born to cuddle. Others just want to hunt. Dog **breeds** may seem vastly different, but they are all from the same family. This is the family **Canidae**.

Dogs descend from another member of the family Canidae, the gray wolf. Historians believe humans first tamed wolf pups to help them hunt. That makes wolves distant relatives of friendly family dogs!

For more than 12,000 years, humans have bred dogs to get ideal features. Some dogs are miniature and can be carried in a purse! Others are large, fierce, and perfect for guard dog work. Still others are bred to hunt specific prey.

The terrier is a good example of this. The word *terrier* comes from the Latin *terra* meaning "earth." Many terriers were **bred** to dig into the ground to catch small prey. One of these is the West Highland white terrier.

The West Highland white terrier is also known as the Westie.

WEST HIGHLAND WHITE TERRIERS

In the past, the terrier's main job was to control the population of rats and other vermin. They dove right into animal holes to capture their prey! Fox hunters also valued these hardy dogs.

The West Highland white terrier originated in Poltalloch, Scotland. There, the Malcolm family raised terriers of various colors.

One day, one of their terriers was mistaken for a fox. It was accidentally shot during a hunt. After that, the Malcolms focused specifically on **breeding** white terriers.

Westies are part of the AKC's terrier group. Most members of this group are originally from the British Isles.

The Westie proved to be the courageous, feisty, easily identifiable dog the Malcolms wanted. The **American Kennel Club (AKC)** first registered the dog under the name Roseneath terrier. It has been shown under the name West Highland white terrier since 1909.

QUALITIES

The West Highland white terrier maintains many of its original qualities. This hardworking **breed** is energetic and loves to dig. It is bold with other dogs, making it seem like a big dog in a small body.

The Westie can also be a barker. It was bred this way so it could be found even when chasing prey underground! With proper training, the Westie can learn to bark only when appropriate.

Indoors, Westies remain energetic and playful. Yet they will sometimes cuddle with family members. Westies are milder than some terriers. So, they can be good with children. If introduced early, other dogs should be fine as well. However, small pets are not a good idea. Westies may see them as prey.

Westies are strong-willed, so owners must show leadership. Westies that think they are in charge have behavior problems such as snapping. Luckily, these dogs are very smart and respond well to training.

In Scotland, Westies hunted foxes and otters on rough terrain. They are still happy to join owners on a hike!

COAT AND COLOR

Dogs in the terrier group range in color. However, the West Highland white terrier is known for its solid white coat. This bright coat has two layers. The undercoat is soft and **dense**. The outer coat consists of straight, hard hair.

The hard white coat is around two inches (5 cm) long on the Westie's trunk. Shorter hair stands on the neck and shoulders. Longer hair hangs from the stomach and legs. To maintain this look, the entire coat requires trimming about every two months.

If the coat appears dull or dirty, a bath will bring back its brilliant white color. Baths should be

The Westie's outer coat repels water. The undercoat keeps the dog warm. Together, they protect these hunting dogs from prey and rough terrain.

occasional. And, owners should use a mild shampoo made especially for dogs. This helps protect the **breed**'s hard coat and sensitive skin.

SIZE

The West Highland white terrier is a small dog. Ideally, males measure 11 inches (28 cm) at the shoulders. Females are slightly smaller. They should be 10 inches (25 cm) tall.

The Westie has a well-balanced body. The **breed** weighs between 15 and 20 pounds (7 and 9 kg). The weight is distributed evenly from the Westie's narrow chest to its strong hindquarters and muscular legs.

The Westie's round head is in proportion to the rest of its body. It features dark brown, almond-shaped eyes. The short **muzzle** ends in a large black nose. The Westie's ears are erect, triangular, and furry like the rest of its adorable face.

Westies aren't just cute and fun. These dogs are smart, confident, and speedy!

CARE

The active Westie needs more exercise than many other dog **breeds**. A long daily walk or a run outdoors keeps him happy and fit! Playing with family and getting groomed also meet the Westie's need for love and attention.

Regular grooming is important for this breed. The Westie **sheds** little. But regular brushing with a firm, wire bristle brush leaves even less hair around the home. And, brushing distributes skin oils. This helps keep the coat and skin healthy.

Nail and teeth care are also key. Avoid scratched furniture and people with regular nail trimming. Brush your dog's teeth several times a week. This keeps teeth healthy and prevents illness. Be sure to use a toothpaste made especially for dogs.

All dogs also need checkups with a trained veterinarian. Veterinarians provide **vaccines** and **spay** or **neuter** pets. They also identify and treat many common Westie health concerns. These include skin, jaw, knee, lung, and liver problems.

Regular grooming allows you to check for health changes in your pet.

15

FEEDING

The spunky West Highland white terrier loves to eat! Its food needs will change over time. Is it a growing puppy, or does it just need to maintain its adult weight? Does it need extra energy for things like **agility** competitions?

Luckily, there are many quality commercial dog foods available. These come in several varieties.

The first and most popular is dry food. It has a long shelf life and helps clean teeth. Many owners combine it with moist or semimoist foods.

Many Westies love to compete! It's a great way to spend time with your pet.

Your Westie will not say no to treats! Just be sure to use them sparingly in order to avoid unhealthy weight gain.

This adds extra flavor and water to dry food.

Puppies between six weeks and six months of age need four small meals of puppy food every day. This is best for small stomachs and rapid growth. Cut back to three meals a day for older puppies. Adult dogs do well with two larger meals per day.

THINGS THEY NEED

Westies do well in large and small homes and in cities and rural areas. They just need enough activity! Otherwise, these sporty dogs become bored. And bored dogs become naughty. To avoid bad behavior, walk or play outside with your pet every day.

Some owners provide multiple beds for their Westies. For example, there might be one bed in a main room and one in a bedroom.

After exercising, a dog crate is a good place for rest. A crate is also useful for training and travel. Add bedding to make it extra cozy.

Other items to have on hand include a leash and a collar with identification tags. Provide sturdy dog dishes and plenty of fresh water. Find safe toys to keep your pet entertained. Lastly, lots of attention makes the Westie a happy dog! These social animals should not be left tied up alone outdoors.

Many Westies also love to swim! Playing fetch is another particularly good activity for these hunting dogs.

PUPPIES

Is that a puppy or a cotton ball? One might ask this of the newborn Westie. A mother Westie is **pregnant** for around 63 days. Then, she usually gives birth to a **litter** of three to five puppies.

Westie puppies are tiny, deaf, and blind at birth. They are completely dependent on their mother for nursing and care.

Some Westies live to be up to 20 years old!

20

After 10 to 14 days, the puppies gain their sight and hearing. Soon after, they begin to explore their world.

Puppies **wean** naturally beginning around six weeks of age. But, they stay close to their mother and the other puppies. This is important for **socialization**.

The darling puppies are ready for their new families after 12 weeks of age. Healthy and happy West Highland white terriers make devoted pets for 12 to 16 years.

For many years, the Westie has ranked in the AKC's top 40 most popular dogs.

GLOSSARY

agility - a sport in which a handler leads a dog through an obstacle course during a timed race.

American Kennel Club (AKC) - an organization that studies and promotes interest in purebred dogs.

breed - a group of animals sharing the same ancestors and appearance. A breeder is a person who raises animals. Raising animals is often called breeding them.

Canidae (KAN-uh-dee) - the scientific Latin name for the dog family. Members of this family are called canids. They include wolves, jackals, foxes, coyotes, and domestic dogs.

dense - thick or compact.

litter - all of the puppies born at one time to a mother dog.

muzzle - an animal's nose and jaws.

neuter (NOO-tuhr) - to remove a male animal's reproductive glands.

pregnant - having one or more babies growing within the body.

shed - to cast off hair, feathers, skin, or other coverings or parts by a natural process.

socialization - adapting an animal to behaving properly around people or other animals in various settings.

spay - to remove a female animal's reproductive organs.

vaccine (vak-SEEN) - a shot given to prevent illness or disease.

wean - to accustom an animal to eating food other than its mother's milk.

WEB SITES

To learn more about West Highland white terriers, visit ABDO Publishing Company online. Web sites about West Highland white terriers are featured on our Book Links page. These links are routinely monitored and updated to provide the most current information available.

www.abdopublishing.com

23

INDEX

24